# FUNDAMENTALS *to* A FULFILLED LIFE

CHIDI GABRIEL UMEH

Fundamentals to a Fulfilled Life by Chidi Gabriel Umeh

This book is written to provide information and motivation to readers. Its purpose is not to render any type of psychological, legal, or professional advice of any kind. The content is the sole opinion and expression of the author, and not necessarily that of the publisher.

Copyright © 2020 by Chidi Gabriel Umeh

All rights reserved. No part of this book may be reproduced, transmitted, or distributed in any form by any means, including, but not limited to, recording, photocopying, or taking screenshots of parts of the book, without prior written permission from the author or the publisher. Brief quotations for noncommercial purposes, such as book reviews, permitted by Fair Use of the U.S. Copyright Law, are allowed without written permissions, as long as such quotations do not cause damage to the book's commercial value.

ISBN: 978-1-952822-88-9 (Paperback)
ISBN: 978-1-952822-87-2 (Digital)

Library of Congress Control Number: 2020920799

Printed in the United States of America.

# PRAISE FOR THE BOOK

This book is one of best books I've read this year. I literally didn't want it to end. It will empower you to live out your best life. The principles in this book are very practical...putting them to work will forever change your life. I recommend this book one hundred percent.

—Marivon Sama
(CEO Zoe Creative Studio)

This book helped me in understanding some key steps I need to take towards living a fulfilled life. I got to reflect on my current state of life and how to proceed with making changes. I strongly believe the best way to digest this book is with an open mind. Lessons shared by the author are evidence that these fundamentals work and are solid foundational essentials for a purpose—driven life.

—Nneka Chukwudozie
(Founder First Steps Initiative)

# CONTENT

**PRAISE FOR THE BOOK** .................................................. iii

**INTRODUCTION** ............................................................ vii

  1:   **PICTURE IT**

       (See with your mind's eye the possibilities) ..................... 1

  2:   **BURY YOUR DOUBT UNDER CONFIDENCE**

       (Doubt cripples dreams) ............................................... 5

  3:   **PURE INTENTIONS**

       (Don't soil the process) ............................................... 9

  4:   **PATIENCE**

       (Key element of success) ............................................. 13

  5:   **GRATITUDE**

       (The wagon of harmony ) ........................................... 17

  6:   **MANAGING YOUR TIME AND FRIENDSHIP**

       (Non-Refundable currency) ......................................... 21

  7:   **MINDSET**

       (Your Anchor to greatness) ......................................... 25

8: DILIGENCE
    (The wheel of productivity) ......................................... 29
9: OBEDIENCE
    (Gateway to Mastery) ................................................ 33
10: KINDNESS
    (Seed of immeasurable returns) ................................ 37
DESERT ............................................................................. 41
ACKNOWLEDGEMENT ....................................................... 45

# INTRODUCTION

The goal of this book is to provide you with the foundational steps necessary to live a fulfilled life. And also help you develop your mind so that you can live your best life. In reading this simple book, I plead with you to pay undivided attention to the ten life-transforming and self-management tips described herein. I guarantee you will catch a word that will spark and ignite something in you that will bring to life your unique abilities and make you a more valuable, fulfilled, and exceptional person on this earth. And most of all, secure you a perfect place for eternity.

In your thoughts you may say; I'm already successful and don't need this book. Well, can you truly say that you are content with your life? Success doesn't equal fulfillment. Success can be traced to a particular area or areas of one's life, but fulfillment is traced to every area of one's life. Meaning, success is just a part of a fulfilled life. There are some simple, yet often neglected self-management skills which a person must employ to actually live a fulfilled life. You can be successful in your career and not be satisfied, you can be successful in your relationships or business, and still not be content. Dr. Myles Munroe said, "True happiness is embedded in what you can become and not what you can get."

It is now an undisputed fact that our attitudes in life are a product of our thoughts and beliefs. If you embrace the ten techniques outlined in this book, which will help you to develop your mind build your character, you will clearly see that you, along with every human on earth, have what it takes to live a fulfilled life.

Fulfillment is not for the rich or the privileged, you can choose to live a meaningful, satisfied life or not. Your fulfillment is anchored on the mindsets you embrace in your life. This simple but great book will challenge you, your beliefs, and your understanding of the characteristics of a successful person you think you may already know.

Be blessed.

CHAPTER

## PICTURE IT

> The only thing that makes life unfair is the delusion that it should be fair.
>
> —DR. STEVEN MARABOLI

Life is fair to anyone that pictures it fair. As little kids our parents or guardian make most decisions like; the type of food we ate, the clothes we wore, the schools we attended and our times of nap and sleep. They even chose our friends, or at the very least suggested friends for us. All these were not just done out of necessity. In our parents' minds, their actions were shaping us into wonderful teenagers and perfect adults. Sometimes it may seem a bit too much for us, but one thing was very clear inside their minds, they were picturing the wonderful future they wanted for us and were doing everything possible from their perspective to make that picture a reality.

This brings us to the first self-management technique: You must abort every thought in your mind that life is unfair and picture yourself achieving your dreams despite the obstacles. It has been established that positive thoughts automatically yield positive attitudes, thereby attracting positive results to your life. When you think, it is possible, then, it becomes possible. You can only be a problem solver, when you have the mentality that there is a solution to every problem even if you haven't found it yet. Martin Luther King Jr. said, "The human heart is like a ship on a stormy sea driven about by winds blowing from all four corners of heaven." When you are yet to discover or find your purpose and are still hunting for your desired future, when you encounter challenges, problems, and turmoil, it is natural to have thoughts rushing in. It may seem like life is unfair to you, that you're not good enough, or that life is for the privileged. Those thoughts are the stormy winds blowing in our minds, but remember you have the power to control those stormy thoughts. We've all had a negative friend, coworker or acquaintance, who can never see the forest for the trees, who always shoots down a great idea or vision by pointing out the obstacles and why it won't work. Wisdom demands that you distance yourself from such people, you can do the same with negative thoughts.

Remember this; you always become what you imagine or think. The question is, what do you have to lose when you picture yourself as a great person, when you see your future as remarkable, when you imagine the enormous positive impact you will make in the world, when you envision your life as legendary? Most people are scared to dream big because of the fear and feelings of disappointment they think they will experience if they fail to actualize their dreams. I'll tell you what; disappointment is not the end, it is only a missed deadline or target, but the good thing is, you can create another opportunity, another objective.

I want to introduce you to a word called CHUTZPAH. Michael Gelb defined CHUTZPAH as a" Yiddish word that can be interpreted to mean audacity and nerve in the face of uncertainty." Life is all about how you picture those uncertainties. The closest word to CHUTZPAH in English is MOXIE; when you've got moxie, you tend to interpret situations differently because you see them from a different perspective. You have to adopt CHUTZPAH as a lifestyle in order to succeed. You have the power to picture things positively, that's how ideas are birthed. Don't allow the devil or your surroundings to control your thoughts. You got this, you can do it, but only when you believe you can.

ENGAGE AND WALK WITH THE WORDS YOU JUST READ, ENGAGE THE HELP OF THE HOLY SPIRIT AND I GUARANTEE YOU; YOUR GREATNESS IS AT YOUR DOOR STEP.

# CHAPTER 2

## BURY YOUR DOUBT UNDER CONFIDENCE

> Confidence comes not from always being right but from not fearing to be wrong.
>
> —PETER T. MCINTYRE

O.G. Mandino said," weak is he who allows all his thoughts to control his actions, and strong is he who allows his actions to control his thoughts." I remember asking myself how is that even possible, I mean you have to think before you act, right? But I have grown to understand that the mind is like a market place where different thoughts struggle to sell themselves, while our actions are the goods we finally bought from that market place. Martin Luther Sr. once said, "You can never keep birds from flying over your head, but you can definitely keep them from building a nest in your hair." We can't keep thoughts, whether positive or negative, from flashing in our minds (the market place), but we can decide on which to buy (to adopt in our lives) and which to leave (abort).

This brings us to what I call "DOUBT". I was thinking about what it is that makes people doubt and I realized that it is not because of their in-capabilities as most people think. It's actually out of fear of the outcome of whatever they are planning to do. Listen, before you engage in anything, you would have thought about it right? Then maybe immediately, or perhaps later on, fear grips you, telling you, are you sure you can do this; are you ready or do you even qualify for this? And just like that, doubt is birthed.

Those ideas came to you initially not withstanding your in-capabilities, right? You thought about it for days, weeks, maybe even months. But as a result of the inquisitive nature of man, you began to think, what could be the outcome of this idea? Will people dive into it? Will it sound so ridiculous? Will they even buy it? All these questions are about the end game of something that has not even started! My question is, who told you that it is humanly possible to know the end of a thing from the beginning? You may have it all planned out, but the end game (outcome) is always where the surprises lay. How can you know the end of something you have not even started?

As a teenager, there was this wonderful girl in my school, Ebere—brilliant, beautiful, and calm. I liked her and wanted to be friends. I had been meaning to talk to her for a while and even had the advantage of seeing her after school and on weekends because she lived just a stone's throw from my place. But to approach her and ask her for friendship was a big deal for me. I would make up my mind that I must talk to her today and upon seeing her, thoughts would start flooding in: am I fluent enough? Am I dressed okay? Do I smell good? Am I cute enough? All these thoughts kept coming and, in the end, I couldn't approach her. The truth is all those thoughts were completely meaningless, the only issue was what her response would be; would she say yes or no? So those thoughts were just a way out or reasons for me not to try. I was already making excuses in case she said no, which means I was indirectly setting up and justifying my failure.

How can you succeed when you are already making excuses for failure? It's like laying a failure foundation and expecting to build a success mansion. The funny part of the story is, Anthony, the guy that later went out with Ebere, was less intelligent and less handsome than me. But you know what Anthony had that I didn't, confidence! So, even if he had doubts, he buried them under confidence. All I needed was to silence that voice of doubt and bury those destructive thoughts under confidence. One may ask, what happens when with all that confidence, the girl still says no? Well it's still great because you tried, you went to talk to her, and she was the one that said no. It wasn't you that rejected yourself even before you got to her, that's what matters. The good news is, there is another girl next door, and the next and the next, with your confidence you will finally find your perfect match. With your confidence you will have the power to try again and again and again until you succeed.

I want you to ask yourself one question, what are the benefits of doubt? Absolutely none! You will never know how good you are at any task until you try it. You cannot be a perfect driver if you have never driven before. It's okay to be turned down or rejected or told no, but make sure you don't reject yourself first. Bury that doubt under confidence.

ENGAGE AND WALK WITH THE WORDS YOU JUST READ, ENGAGE THE HELP OF THE HOLY SPIRIT AND I GUARANTEE YOU; YOUR GREATNESS IS AT YOUR DOOR STEP.

# CHAPTER 3

## PURE INTENTIONS

*A heart with pure intentions will never lead you astray.*

—NANCY D'SOUZA

It is well established that every human has intentions towards life or towards any particular task, the question is how pure are your intentions? do your intentions in life serve a greater purpose than you or is it just about you and your immediate family? When the going gets tough will you still remain true to your purpose or will you adulterate your process. Pure means unadulterated, uncontaminated, or unpolluted, while intention means an aim or plan, purpose or target or an objective. Now pure intention means unadulterated, uncontaminated, unpolluted plan, aim or purpose. A great man of God I know Bishop David Oyedepo said, "If you don't live for something, you don't become something." In other words, if you don't live for a purpose, you can't achieve one. Dr. Myles Munroe in one of his quotes stated, "When purpose is not known, abuse is inevitable." When you can't figure out your purpose here on earth, you are bound to be abused, trampled upon, and under live your life; you live at the mercy of other people. You will constantly feel incapable, undeserved and that always leads to several abuse, and harassment.

I'll tell you what, some people go through this abuse, rejection, and harassment, not because they haven't found their purpose, but because they have contaminated or polluted the process and themselves in pursuit of this purpose. Their purpose is of no value anymore even to them, because they have darkened their soul and soiled their hands in pursuit of this intention, purpose, or goal. When I themed this chapter pure intentions, I understood the fact that many people upon the face of the earth have intentions about life, the problem is always how pure will they remain in pursuit of those intentions, how true will they stay to the process. It might be pure at first, but what happens when the journey begins, when challenges set in and difficulties kept knocking and throwing stones? Will you contaminate your process and yourself or will you stay true to yourself and the process? The truth is; is not as easy as it sounds. I have witnessed many great men fell because they exchanged handshakes with the devil during their process. Before the end of this chapter, I will give you tips on how to stay true and pure to yourself and towards your goal. A goal can never be attained and a purpose can never be achieved without a process, and that process is what always defines your purpose, or let me say that process is what gives your purpose a meaning. A certain young man got a job at a great pharmaceutical company, he worked so hard, he had all the right work ethics and did almost everything right. This young man had an intention of gaining a director position one day or even owning his own company, and that is a very good intention, plus he is working hard for it. Then some years later, he had these groups of friends that he normally hanged out with, now these friends started saying stuffs to him jokingly. They called him "Mr. Workaholic, they mocked him for working so hard and giving the company his best but has nothing in return." Of course, this young man had been awarded several benefits and rewards. But his friends always made that joke around him, and as time went on this young man began to think about those things and began to be demoralized. He was very smart so he began to think how to manipulate things to get the position that he wanted. He works hard now not unto good works to achieve his intentions, but on how to deceitfully get to the director position.

I want you to understand this very well, this young man still has his intention of becoming a director in his company which is a good intention, but the process to achieve that intention has shifted, the process is polluted. He still has his intention, but they are no longer pure. To have a goal or purpose in life matters, but what matters most is how pure is the process to that purpose. Remember your goal becomes meaningless and valueless even when you achieve them through an impure or polluted process. These tips will help you to keep a pure intention:

1. Walk in love: you need to embrace the liberty of your soul and spirit, express love and share it and hope for nothing in return.
2. Be open minded: you need openness of heart. Be ever willing to adjust to Godly instructions, even if they contradict your desires.
3. Be interested more in what you have to offer or services you have to render than the rewards. Believe you are created for a higher purpose bigger than you, so every one of your actions will be towards that higher purpose not for rewards.
4. Place service and stewardship before and above profit or gain. Embrace servant hood and love it, especially if you are in leadership position.

5. Always be joyful: Have a heart full of joy and live a joyful life. Proverbs 17:22 says, "A joyful heart is a good medicine." A joyful heart destroys bad intents. It keeps you from creating room to feel undeserved. Joyful heart makes you immune to hate. Recall I always use joy not happiness, because joy comes from within, happiness can be tied or traced to a particular thing which could be temporary. That is not enough, you need joy and you can only get this joy when you connect to God and help humanity.

Pure intentions produce pure results!

ENGAGE AND WALK WITH THESE WORDS YOU JUST READ, AND ENGAGE THE HELP OF THE HOLY SPIRIT AND I GUARANTEE YOU; YOUR GREATNESS IS AT YOUR DOOR STEP.

CHAPTER

# PATIENCE

Patience is not the ability to wait, but the ability to keep a good attitude while waiting.

—JOYCE MEYER

William Langland stated, "patience is a virtue." William Henry Gates III popularly known as Bill Gates says, "patience is a key element of success." Now biblically the quality of patience is presented as either forbearance or endurance. We all understand from the dictionary definition that patience is the capacity to accept or tolerate delay, trouble or suffering without getting angry or frustrated. In our world today many people don't consider patience as a virtue. Everyone wants instant results. There is nothing wrong with having instant results to a thing or instant solution to a problem as long as you can find a positive answer. We are going to explore in this chapter, how we can use this powerful tool called patience. Note this: the duration of any particular task differs from another and so the process, application, and method of an individual towards any given task differs too. Trust me on this, you have to know the why behind your waiting or the value of the task ahead before your waiting can be worth something. The quality of patience can only fully be appreciated when an individual knows the reason for the delay or the value of the task.

I recalled the first day I went for my driving class, I got there twenty minutes early, the class was supposed to start by 9:00am. Some other students were already there, while some came later, but something happened. We were supposed to start by 9:00am but we waited till 9:30am and yet the teacher had not yet arrived. People began to get furious and angry; some were complaining aggressively, others couldn't wait and they walked out. I myself was angry too, but I couldn't walk away, because that task held so much value to me at that time. Not only did I want to learn the principles of driving, my wife was pregnant with our first child and was due in four months. I needed this class so I could be able to drove her around because of her condition. I was angry because I didn't know the reason for the wait or delay, but I was patient because that task was valuable to me at that time. Many more walked out, and some were complaining loudly and aggressively. About 10:15am a certain gentleman walked up to us and asked, "Are you all here for the driving class?" With anger and frustration everyone shouted" Yes!" Then he said, "I am so sorry to inform you guys, but I just got a call this morning that your teacher got into an accident this morning while on his way to class. We thank God he is alright, he only sustained little bruises, but the car was totally damaged. Everyone was calm, we stared at each other, especially people that were saying bad stuff about the teacher, there was sudden calmness in the environment. The reason was not because the teacher was involved in an accident, of course everyone that stayed felt sorry for him. The reason for the calmness was because amidst all the delay, anger, and frustration, we found out the reason we were kept waiting for over an hour.

What I am saying is, always know the value of the task you are been patient about and weigh the task value against the waiting period to determine if it is worth it. The reason I waited was because I knew how valuable that task was to me and my family, it is not just about me, it was beyond me. My wife was involved, and my unborn baby. You have to think of how it affects others too, not just you, that's what makes it valuable. Remember some individuals walked away. We were all there for the same task, but the task didn't hold the same value for all of us. You may have a goal that you are chasing, a career path, or an idea in your head waiting to be born. The process between your starting point and actualization of that goal, dream, career or business idea is where the tool patience is needed. The question is how valuable is this goal to you? You have to identify how valuable and important this goal is to you and how it affects others. Many had abandoned their ideas and goals that would have brought about a great positive change to this world, only because they got tired of waiting, they were inpatient about the process. I always tell people the waiting process is the refining process. When we understand the value of that task, when we understand that giving up on that ideas or goals or whatever it is we are pursuing, is actually doing a disservice to humanity, we will embrace this tool called patience and run with it.

When we learn to embrace patience, it becomes a virtue for us. Remember between the planting or sowing seasons and the harvest seasons, there is always a waiting period and those waiting periods should be cherished cause you are sure of your harvest. Right now I challenge you to go back to that idea or goal or whatever it is you abandoned because you think you can't continue, that book you were writing, that business you wanted to start, that dream home and family you have always wanted, with what you have learned about patience, you can make it work, you can bring that into existence, you can make it a reality. Just do it.

ENGAGE AND WALK WITH THESE WORDS YOU JUST READ, AND ENGAGE THE HELP OF THE HOLY SPIRIT AND I GUARANTEE YOU; YOUR GREATNESS IS AT YOUR DOOR STEP.

CHAPTER

## GRATITUDE

> Gratitude turns what we have into enough, and more. It turns Denial into acceptance, chaos into order, confusion into clarity... It makes sense of our past, brings peace for today, and creates A vision for tomorrow.
>
> —MELODY BEATTIE

Gratitude is an attitude, in other words it is a character or a habit, which means it can be learned, cultivated, and developed. Gratitude does not come naturally; you have to learn it. It is an act of being grateful and showing appreciation for any good or kindness shown to you by God or by any man. As easy as it may seem, it is very difficult for many people to show gratitude or be thankful; Why? because gratitude and thankfulness can only be meaningful when it comes from the heart. Gratitude is the quality of being thankful and readiness to show appreciation and ability to return kindness. The act of saying thank you to a person, or people, when they show you support, a favor, or kindness is not what gratitude is all about.

This is very important, there are habits {I call them virtues} that you must have to truly be a grateful person or to truly have a heart of gratitude. They are meekness and love, without these two you can't truly be grateful, you can only fake it. Gratitude is not just an act of being thankful it is the quality of your thankfulness. So, your show of gratitude must possess quality, it mustn't just be an act, but it must possess value to make it meaningful and acceptable. A humble or meek person appreciates whatever help is rendered to him or her no matter how small it is, but a proud person degrades gifts, help, or any other form of assistance shown to him or her. They may say thank you but their heart is saying otherwise. When you sincerely love people, not withstanding their race, background, or color, you are always grateful and appreciative of any little thing they do for you or any assistance they rendered to you. The truth is; before you learn how to say thank you or how to be grateful, you need to learn first how to love and how to be meek or humble, otherwise your gratitude is insignificant, which makes it ingratitude in return.

In the words of Henry Ward Beecher, "Gratitude is the fairest blossom which springs from the soul". It is a heart thing; it must be from your soul. One might be thinking, "Why do I need to show gratitude even to a person below my class" or a nobody like we popularly say. Understand this; to be truly thankful to someone actually does not much good or holds not much benefit to the person you are thanking. You have almost all the benefits to enjoy. Saying thank you to someone that rendered you help or assistance gives them a sense of happiness and satisfaction that they are being appreciated, but it opens you up for more benefits, it improves both your physical and psychological health, it gives you peace of mind. It reduces your emotional stress; it kills depression and self-rejection. The fact that somebody loves you, and care enough to render you any form of assistance or help, not minding how little it may seem, that will give you mental strength. Remember no form of help or gift is considered small: someone holding the door for you to pass, someone assisting you with your projects or assignments, someone buying you bottled water, financial assistance, whatever help it is, you should learn or cultivate the habit of saying thank you sincerely. When you come home after the day's work, you thank God for the day, when you sleep and wake up the next morning, you should say thank you to God.

When you eject the clutters in your heart, it helps you be thankful. Marcel Proust said, "Let us be grateful to the people who make us happy; they are the charming gardeners who make our soul blossom" just think on these words for a bit. Ralph Waldo Emerson also stated, "Cultivate the habit of being grateful for every good thing that comes to you, and to give thanks continuously. And because all things have contributed to your advancement, you should include all things in your gratitude." You need peace of mind in order to be at your best, you need peace in order to be creative and effective, and gratitude offers that peace. Remember gratitude is worth nothing without humility and love. John Ortberg said, "Gratitude is the ability to experience life as a gift. It liberates us from the prison of self- preoccupation". You don't only thank people when they render help or give you a gift, you also thank people when they want to help but don't have the resources to do so, you thank them for their intentions to help, you thank them for loving you and thinking about you. Gratitude gives joy both to the giver and receiver. Amy Collette said, "Gratitude is a powerful catalyst for happiness. It's the spark that lights a fire of joy in your soul". The amount of your achievements or success in life doesn't always depend on your hard works, many times it is traced back to your quality of thankfulness. Gratitude attracts favor before God and before man.

ENGAGE AND WALK WITH THESE WORDS YOU JUST READ, AND ENGAGE THE HELP OF THE HOLY SPIRIT AND I GUARANTEE YOU; YOUR GREATNESS IS AT YOUR DOOR STEP.

## CHAPTER 6

## MANAGING YOUR TIME AND FRIENDSHIP

You are the average of the five people you spend the most time with.

—JIM ROHN

Pastor David Ibiyeomie, the founder of salvation ministries would often say, "The company you keep determines what will accompany you." The author of Walking Through the Parallel of an Individual Cell, Kenneth G. Ortiz comments, "Be wary of the company you keep for they are a reflection of who you are, or who you want to be... This is very important; it is impossible to separate your time from your relationships with friends or family. Every friendship is built on time, so these two things work together. The foundation of any lasting relationship or friendship is trust, not love. You can actually love someone but not trust them, just like kids, you love them but can't trust them because of their ignorance of the dangers around them. Love is still vital in friendships or relationships, but trust is the foundation. And to build trust takes TIME. The issue of a wrong friendship has ruined so many destinies and has turned some people with great potentials to failures. This is very important, never make friends unconsciously, or subconsciously, there should be a very steady high wall when it comes to who you let in in your life, if you really want to amount to something meaningful in life. It has nothing to do with pride, it's called being careful.

There is something very significant about friendship or relationships as the case may be. When you call someone your friend, they occupy a place in your heart subconsciously, which means you think about them even when they are not with you, knowingly or unknowingly. I can equivocally say that; they become part of you. The good part is, if they influence you positively, your subconscious mind automatically starts to absorb those qualities, but the bad part is, if they are a negative influence the same thing happens. This is the reason why making friends intentionally and consciously is very important, am not saying chase people away, am saying don't let everyone in. when you love people you share things with them, when you trust people you share secrets with them, you share ambitions, goals, ideas. When you have a friend that you love and trust, he or she automatically has a place in your heart, which means any habit or opinion from him or her subconsciously settles on the ground of your heart in which they occupy, thereby influencing your thoughts and actions unknowingly. And that could be good or bad. If you want to manage your time well, you have to manage your friendships first, it's very important. Every friendship affects time and time is the thread upon which every activity hangs on.

Many have misunderstood this statement; "choose friends that are more successful than you" and they think that they have to visually make or choose friends that are more successful than them, or people who had already been where they want to go, in order for them to be influenced, promoted, or successful. That's true, but not completely true, I think the first thing to look out for when choosing friends is their moral standard. Many successful people lack this. They are materially successful but their spiritual life and morality is nothing to write home about, when you associate yourself with the type I just described, you might eventually be successful materially but your moral life will be a mess just like them. One of the things to look out for when making friends is the zeal and the passion that drives them, they don't necessarily need to already be successful, you just need to identify what motivates them, what are they passionate about, what is their mindset, what are they focused on, what consumes their time the most, with this, you know where they are headed.

There are many successful people with questionable characters. Look out for positivity not just wealth. Look for friends that use their intangible wealth to secure tangible wealth. You might say it doesn't matter, all I care about is becoming wealthy, I tell you it matters. Time will reveal all things. What happens when you get all that wealth and you still remain unfulfilled and unhappy? Also, remember that not all mentors are healthy for friendship, you need to identify the line between mentorship and friendship. Choose your friends consciously and also choose your mentors consciously. Do not just make friends based on physical achievements and possessions, make friends with a healthy and a positive mindset, a healthy mindset is a wealthy mindset. No matter how your friends influence you, positively or negatively, the consequences are still yours to bear. So, don't just choose good friends, choose the right ones, the right friend helps you manage your time wisely, because they place value on every second of their time. The one tip to manage your time effectively and efficiently is, never place a task on yourself, place the task on your time. Let your time work for you, that way you make your time valuable. Value is what makes you relevant, the value you possess makes you unavoidably important, so make friends with value.

One may be wondering, "how can I identify the right friends?" First thing; find out how they spend their time, that is very important. Jim Rohn would say, "Don't spend major time on minor things", the people you associate with, do they spend major time on minor things? What are they passionate about? You must consider these things before letting them in, is ok to have casual friends provided you only give them casual time and attention. Perhaps you already have friends in your life, who are negatively affecting the quality of your life, the solution is disassociation. Limit the time you spend with them until you completely get rid of them. It sounds mean but if you truly want to impact lives, lead a successful and fulfilled life, and if you care about your priorities and values, you will let them go. The truth is, it is impossible to associate yourself with negative friends and expect to be successful in life.

ENGAGE AND WALK WITH THESE WORDS YOU JUST READ, AND ENGAGE THE HELP OF THE HOLY SPIRIT AND I GUARANTEE YOU; YOUR GREATNESS IS AT YOUR DOOR STEP.

CHAPTER

# MINDSET

You don't need a new day to start over, you only need a new mindset.

—HAZEL HIRA OZBEK

It is very important for us to understand truly what a mindset is. Motivational speakers and mentors have always talked about mindset. They have always admonished us to have a positive mindset in order to become great or relevant in our pursuit of our life goal or purpose. But it is very important that we first truly understand what mindset is. The best way to make something effective is to find the root cause of what is making that same thing not effective and then tackle it. So, in this chapter, I will be breaking down the word MINDSET, so everyone will really understand what a mindset is, thereby knowing how to engage the power of mindset. The dictionary defines the mind as "the element of a person that enables them to be aware of the world and their experiences, to think and to feel." While the mindset is the established set of all those experiences, environment, awareness, circumstances and values. Underline the word "established set" in this sentence. I define mindset as the sum total of your ideologies, that is, your belief system and the factors that inform the decisions you make. That's why environments, value systems, and belief systems affect the mindset. Example: the mindset of someone that grew up in the United States is different from one who grew up in Ghana. The mindset of a person who grew up in an abusive environment is different someone who grew up in an environment of love and care. The good thing is mindset can be changed. It has been established that a man can never rise above his mindset, because the foundation of his mindset is based on the factors that his environment, value, and belief system has formed around him. Later in this chapter I will be teaching on how to overcome that.

I want to give you a definition of mindset that will help you be in better control of your mind. Never look at your mind as an element of a person. NO! See your mind as a person, see your mind as the smarter and exposed version of you, with all the same organs you have in your body present in the mind person. The mind is that you in the middle. It makes you a dual citizen of both the unseen world and the real world, you can call it the spiritual and the earth realm. The mind has the ability to travel both realms, it is the advanced version of you. Your mind has the capacity to travel to your future and create things and then come back to your present version of you and instill the factors and values in you that will make that future a reality. But note this: your mind can only do that when you train it to. That is why I said your mind is a person, so it grows too. The information your mind gathers from the future you and from different places and things is what is used to create that "established set" {mindset}. I want you to read these words again slowly and carefully for you to understand it. This is the reason why you will see somebody from a third-world country making waves and impacting lives more than someone in a new world, because he or she has trained their minds to travel far and wide to gather knowledge and information.

Know this, no matter how daft you think you are, no matter how timid, uncivilized and/or unprivileged you think you are, the person of your mind is better, smarter, more advanced than your present version. It has the capacity to possess, process, and establish knowledge, information and values from your future and from anywhere only when you train and allow it.

These steps will help you train your mind as a person; your mindset:

Engage the Holy Spirit of God: The Holy Spirit is a person too; He is one of the trinity in one God. He is the most intelligent entity upon the face of the planets. You can actually talk and communicate with Him, but first you have to seek Him, then find Him before you can talk with Him. You don't have to be a graduate or a professor to seek Him, you don't need to be rich or living in a new world country to find Him. You can seek Him wherever and however you are, all you need is a sincere heart and you will find Him. He can program the mind person and show you things to come. He can help your mindset to be positive and effective, and will also help to pass the realities of your mind to your present version.

Embrace positive knowledge: this is very important, you can't train your mind as a person when you don't read, study and seek knowledge through books, tapes, courses, biographies, etc. Remember your mind is a person, it needs to grow just like your physical body needs growth. The body needs food, water, and nutrients to grow, while the mind needs knowledge and information to grow. Just as the physical growth comes with the development of your sensitive organs, so is the mind when it grows, the organs for sensitivity become sharper and more active.

Be open to change and adapt to growth. There is always a pathway to success and it is not always comfortable. Be open to change when necessary, embrace growth by learning always, seek directions and Guidance from morally sound successful people that have gone ahead of you. It doesn't necessarily mean you have to meet them in person. You can follow and study people without meeting them in person. Those people have passed through that part of life and came out successful and great. So, it is a certainty, and nothing gives confidence and guarantees success and dignity like certainty. Certainty gives the person of your mind flight.

Never accept failure: Acceptance is something that has to do with the heart and the mind person get destabilized when failure is accepted. See any failed event as a refining moment. That alone empowers the mind person that it is making progress, just like when you thank and appreciate someone, they will want to do more, so will the mind person. Remember the mind as a person has already travelled to see the possibilities of your future. Since it is the advanced version of you, if he can see those possibilities, it is achievable. The unfolding phases of every aspect of our lives and destinies should be cherished not feared. Failure is refusing to try new things for the fear of the unknown.

You can learn how to communicate and manage your mind as a person, that way you make the best use of your mind. Your mind has the tendency to become smarter when you are faced with difficulties. The billionaire, Jon Huntsman said; "when facing severe challenges, your mind is normally at its sharpest." When you understand how to groom the sensitive organs of the mind person, you become extremely effective.

> ENGAGE AND WALK WITH THESE WORDS YOU JUST READ, AND ENGAGE THE HELP OF THE HOLY SPIRIT AND I GUARANTEE YOU; YOUR GREATNESS IS AT YOUR DOOR STEP.

# CHAPTER 8

## DILIGENCE

Diligence overcomes difficulties; Sloth makes them.

—BENJAMIN FRANKLIN

"What we hope to do with ease, we must learn first to do with diligence." By a poet and playwright, Samuel Johnson. The word diligence has been a bit of a problem to younger generation. We all understood diligence as an act of always been careful and persistent with our work or efforts, and the ability to do things thoroughly and well. I do not doubt this definition, but the same definition is what has put or kept many young people in frustration and doubt over their capabilities and dedication. I want to thoroughly and with all carefulness shift the mind of people to truly understand what this word diligence means. I believe this will make millions of people overcome that definition of diligence that has kept them in disbelief and doubt over their capabilities and cause frustrations. People see diligence or rather a diligent man as a hard-working person, well; let me start by saying this; there is no adult that is not hard working, I know that might sound absurd, but before you say that, just ask yourself what am I working hard towards? The question isn't if you are hard working or not, the question is what are you working hard towards? People work hard towards irrelevant things; many people work so hard not to miss a television program not even by one minute. Others work hard not to miss Friday's night club, you will be amazed how many people work hard towards unreasonable things, things that add no value to their lives. To sit down and watch television for hours is hard work especially all the night, because when you get only few hours of sleep, you feel the same fatigue with someone who has been up late studying or working. So, both of you worked hard last night being awake but the difference is towards what? Being hard working doesn't guarantee you success, please note this: the amount of time, work, energy you channeled to any particular task either makes you successful in that task or makes you productive towards somebody else's success. The reason I said hard work doesn't guarantee your success is when you focus your hard work, energy and time in doing the wrong task, although it might make somebody else successful, it may only make you productive in some cases. Success is the accomplishment of your desired aims or purpose, not someone else's desired aim or purpose. When you are extremely hard working in the wrong task or let me say other people's task you will only be part of a success story not the success itself. In this explanation, I am in no way implying or encouraging you not to work hard for your company or someone else. Of course, they will fire you if you don't. This explanation is for the purpose of better understanding on the subject matter "diligence".

It is very important that we understand that diligence doesn't have to do with work alone, there are other dimensions in life that we require diligence in order to succeed. You can be diligent in your family life, academics, spiritual life, business or career, and so on. When you understand this, you will know that diligence doesn't have to do with careful hard work only. Diligence is the quality of your effectiveness and how you maximize time towards a given or a particular task or tasks. It is not just your productivity, hard work, or the result of a task. It is about the qualities applied towards that productivity, hard work, and task. Those qualities are what makes a man diligent, those qualities are; strategic planning {I call it purpose filled planning}, relentless pursuit, resilience and consistency, endurance, morals, and values. Most times you can see a man working very hard in his job or business but his family life is in disarray. This is also applicable to women. You can't call such a person diligent. You can't be a perfect family man or woman if your management of finances is shabby, you are not diligent. Your spiritual life can't be on a zero growth and you call yourself diligent just because you think you are successful materially. Diligence is a circle that consists of different qualities that apply to different dimensions of life and humanity. In other words, I can tell you to show me a diligent man or woman and I will show you a fulfilled human. Now do not think or believe that it is then very difficult to be diligent, because you have to be perfect. NO! That is a wrong thought or belief. Dr. Johnson said, "few things are impossible to diligence and skill. Great works are performed not by strength, but perseverance." And if you will recall I mentioned consistency and endurance in those qualities. Consistency is the ability to weary or frustrate failure till you succeed. So careful hard work is not diligence, it is a pathway to growing to be diligent. Note this: Amateurism and mistakes are allowed in the pathway to diligence. A diligent man is a successful man and success is overcoming many failures. So, failing doesn't disqualify you from being diligent, provided you never quit. William Shakespeare stated, "That which ordinary men are fit for, I am qualified in. and the best of me is diligence". One of the major things that help people become diligent is purpose. Define what you want or expect in different areas of your life and know your purpose. It doesn't matter how long you have worked for that company, all the late nights, hard work, energy and time, if you are not fulfilled, it means you are not living a purposeful life. You have to make that decision today and right now. WHAT DO YOU TRULY WANT? I don't care how long you have been in that relationship. If you are not happy and fulfilled on the inside, you need to walk away now. Remember a U-turn to the right path is not a failure.

Diligence is a must have quality required to be successful in life, and if your hard work, time, and energy, are channeled at the wrong relationships, wrong jobs or careers, wrong businesses, or professions, then you can never be diligent. That means you can't be successful. Also, those who have tried many things and have failed, like business, relationships, and so on, take a break and engage strategic planning. Study relentlessly towards that path or business you intend to follow or invent and ask the Holy Spirit, the most intelligent entity, for help. You will succeed. Failure when not accepted or allowed to demoralize, automatically impacts faith.

> ENGAGE AND WALK WITH THESE WORDS YOU JUST READ, AND ENGAGE THE HELP OF THE HOLY SPIRIT AND I GUARANTEE YOU; YOUR GREATNESS IS AT YOUR DOOR STEP.

CHAPTER

# OBEDIENCE

> Obedience is the only validation of your salvation, It is the only possible proof that you really recognize the lordship of Jesus Christ.
>
> —JOHN MACARTHUR

To many Christians, the word obedience has been simplified so cheaply that the significant value of obedience has been neglected. Many Christians fail to realize that obedience holds the same value, if not more value than prayer. There are people through the act of obedience became great and successful; the likes of Abraham- see Gen 12: 1-4; Isaac – see Gen 26:2-6, 12-14, also Gideon- judges 6: -35, and there are many more others. Many Christians have become so familiar with God that they normalize disobedience, they always use the phrase "God understands." This is one of the deadly strategies the devil is using to rob many people of their greatness. In some parts of the world, people regard absolute obedience as weakness and in other parts of the world they see it as slavery. Well, in all sense of definition I am not talking about obedience under duress or agreeing to perform any given task under a brutalized atmosphere or environment. I am talking about willingly compliance or submissive to an order or authority and that includes oneself. The French medieval scholar and commentator Shlomo Yitzchaki, generally known by the acronym Rashi {1040-1105} said, "Obeying from love is better than to obey from fear." Yes! Most times people find it easy to obey rules or laws that have punishments meted out when disobeyed. They only obey out of fear, not love. Obeying an instruction or rule simply because of fear of punishment for disobedience, or rather any obedience that has its root built on fear of punishment for disobedience is simply called carefulness, not obedience. You are just being careful to avoid punishment.

Obedience has 3 major qualities: integrity, commitment, and selflessness. One without these 3 qualities can never truly be obedient. I mentioned earlier that obedience is willing compliance to instructions and rules including your own rule. Sometimes we find it difficult to obey or keep our own rules simply because no one punishes us for it, but we fail to realize that disobedience to our own rules will most times cause damage to the people around us. This is where selflessness comes in. It is actually more powerful and profitable to obey than to sacrifice. As a youth, there are certain rules that when you place them upon yourself and obey them, it doesn't just benefit you and shape you into a successful person, it benefits your parents, siblings and even friends. When you decide as a teenager that you are not going to go into drinking, smoking, and doing drugs, and things like that and you stand by that decision, it does something to your parents. It brings them joy, peace and comfort. It takes away frustration, shame, and anxiety from you. All these, is because of obedience. Obedience is a virtue every human should pursue with all tenacity. It is a habit that must be developed.

Parents also don't make rules and regulations for your children and not keep those same rules simply because no one will punish you if you don't. That is where integrity comes in. You can't tell your child not to smoke while you smoke. You can't tell your child not to drink while you come home drunk almost all the time. You think you are an adult and you can handle yourself, but that is not completely true, you need to obey your own rules for the sake of your children. You don't understand the damage you cause to those children both physically and psychologically, you need integrity and selflessness. Obedience doesn't just benefit you but also people around you, so disobedience doesn't just destroy you but also people around you. The price or reward for obedience is golden and priceless, and the price for disobedience is grievous and deadly.

In the world we live in today everyone wants freedom to do anything they want. They think obedience is such a burden. NO! It is actually the true freedom. OBEDIENCE LEADS TO TRUE FREEDOM. Believers today have become so familiar with God, that they choose the rules to obey and the ones not to. Sincerely speaking, that is wrong. There are certain situations we may find ourselves in life and the answer is not in prayers, praise, or giving or sacrifice, but in a singular act of obedience to a particular instruction. Because it is uncomfortable for us to obey, we tend to sweep it under the carpet. This is where commitment comes in. When you are committed to God, as a Christian, you obey Him effortlessly. For example, the story of Prophet Elisha and the commander of the king's army in Syria, Naaman; 2 kings 5:10-14. Naaman only obeyed the instruction of the prophet by dipping himself seven times in the muddy river Jordan and his leprosy left him, his flesh became clean and younger like a youth. That instruction was very uncomfortable for him, but he obeyed and got his priceless reward. Elisha never forced him to do it, he decided to do it. A great man of God I know, Bishop David Oyedepo said, "Obedience is one of the things that launches the believer into the realm of praying without utterance." In other words, it means obedience is a silent prayer that commands great results.

Remember obedience is vital for you to be very successful in life, you obey to succeed, you don't succeed to obey. Even in your areas of profession you need to adhere to the rules and regulations that guide or govern that establishment in order to excel in your field. In your business, you have rules that govern the business. You can't keep breaking those rules or skipping them and expect your business to grow and expand. Even in your academics and relationships the same rules of obedience are required for you to be academically successful and also have a sweet long-lasting relationship. It is established beyond reasonable doubts that obedience should be a way of life, not just a thing you apply occasionally. A huge part of our success hangs on our ability to obey instructions and rules. Obedience gives our life a meaning and also brings the crown. So, let's stop viewing obedience as denial of freedom, but expression of true freedom. When you develop obedience as a lifestyle, you are truly free. But understand that you need grace in order to be very obedient. Ask God for that grace and he will give you.

ENGAGE AND WALK WITH THESE WORDS YOU JUST READ, AND ENGAGE THE HELP OF THE HOLY SPIRIT AND I GUARANTEE YOU; YOUR GREATNESS IS AT YOUR DOOR STEP.

CHAPTER

# KINDNESS

> Wherever there is a human in need, there is an opportunity for kindness and to make a difference.
>
> —KEVIN HEATH

The word KINDNESS is very deep, it seems so simple and easy but it is not. In the mind of an average person when you mention the word kindness, it sounds so smooth and soft that they don't feel any pressure. However, when you mention sacrifice, it sounds so heavy and difficult and puts pressure on the person right? The fact is; these two words, kindness and sacrifice, can't be separated. You must be sacrificial to be truly kind. In other words, sacrifice and kindness works hand-in-hand. We understand kindness as the quality of being friendly, generous, and considerate. Another definition of kindness says," sincerely and voluntarily using one's time, talent, and resources to better the lives of others, one's own life, and the world through genuine acts of love, compassion, generosity and service." All these definitions indicate or show that kindness is a choice. What is choice? Choice is an act of selecting or making a decision when faced with two or more possibilities. It simply means kindness is an act we choose to render or not when we are faced with a situation that requires our act of kindness. Well, that is not the definition I am bringing into this chapter. Remember I said you can't actually be truly kind without sacrifice. And what is sacrifice one may ask? The oxford dictionary defines it as, "An act of surrendering a possession as an offering to God or to a divine or supernatural figure." Simply what sacrifice means is: offering up a tangible thing or surrendering one's comfort to someone or something greater than you for a purpose bigger than you. If kindness involves sacrifice, it means kindness is not a choice. When you understand that the act of kindness is for a purpose greater than you, you will understand that it is not a choice. Kindness makes the universe a better place, and one of the reasons you and I were created is to better this world. So, it is an obligation we owe both to God and mankind to show kindness to others, the world, and ourselves. It is not a choice. Come to think of it, whenever you show kindness to someone, you will observe that it brings you joy, gives your mind peace and a sense of satisfaction. In the words of the German mathematician and physicist Albert Einstein, "The ideals which have lighted my way, and time after time have given me new courage to face life cheerfully, have been Kindness, Beauty, & Truth".

So, I define kindness as an act of sincerely and sacrificially using one's time, talent, and resources to help or better the lives of others, the world, and yourself. Another attribute that is associated with kindness is compassion. You can't separate kindness from compassion. H. Swanepoel, who is a Raktivist, puts it this way, "Kindness is love made visible". This is where many people fail it. They only show kindness to people from whom they expect something in return. Just like a young man giving a lady a lift or helping her to fix her car simply because he wants to have sex with her. Some people only render help to those they believe can return it. Well, that's wrong. Kindness is love made visible. It means compassion goes in the heart before the act of kindness comes. When you only show kindness to those whom you expect to return it, that is a trade, not kindness. Kindness must possess sacrifice and compassion. You don't have to be rich or have too much to show kindness. Kindness is an attitude; you develop it rich or poor. It doesn't take material possession to be a kind person, it only takes character. Being kind is who you are or who you choose to become. It is not measured by what you have. When you help an elderly person pick up his or her cane, that's an act of kindness and you don't need to be rich to do it. Kindness has little or nothing to do with material possession, it has everything to do with character and principles.

Guy Raz the host of NPR'S "How I built this" said in one of his interviews with "CNBC Make it" he said; with most of the great billionaires he interviewed, he found out that "the key to their success isn't just work ethic and resiliency, that successful entrepreneurs share an incredibly under-rated quality" KINDNESS. He also said, "the return on the investment in kindness is enormous." If you run a kind company and you are a kind entrepreneur and you are collaborative, you will retain your employees. People will work hard to innovate for you and your ideas.

Being kind doesn't just help you to be successful, it makes you impactful. From all ramifications there is really nothing to lose from being kind to people, especially when you understand that it is not just for them, it is for a greater purpose, bigger than you and them. You don't expect your rewards from them, your rewards comes from God.

A good example of someone who showed a complete definition of kindness is JESUS CHRIST. He left His position in heaven and came to earth because of compassion towards mankind. Isaiah 6:8. Because of His compassion towards man, He sacrificed His life on the cross of Calvary to save mankind. That is the height of kindness anyone could offer. Jesus did all that for a higher purpose bigger than Him and mankind. He did not expect a reward from any man but from God His Father. Jesus showed all the qualities embedded in kindness: compassion and sacrifice. And this is worth emulating. I want you to take this to heart: kindness takes you to higher levels in life. You know why? Because you are fulfilling a higher and greater purpose bigger than yourself. Kindness makes you immune to frustration and depression. It is never too late to start showing kindness to people, you can start right here and right now. Turn to whoever is sitting or standing next to you and say nice things to them and watch them smile even if you don't know them. If no one is sitting close to you say nice things to yourself and smile. If you just did that, let me ask you; how did you feel? Keep on practicing it, it pays to be kind to people and to yourself, because it automatically makes you a person of influence. Bob Kerry said;" Unexpected kindness is the most powerful, least costly, and most underrated agent of human change".

ENGAGE AND WALK WITH THESE WORDS YOU JUST READ, AND ENGAGE THE HELP OF THE HOLY SPIRIT AND I GUARANTEE YOU; YOUR GREATNESS IS AT YOUR DOOR STEP.

# DESERT

I observed that many people indeed have tried to develop themselves but their minds are cluttered with many irrelevant things like; anger, un-forgiveness, envy, and so on. What you have just read are foundations that will automatically uncluttered your mind and spirit when you practice them. Thereby making you truly free and empty to take more positivity in, the essence of this book is to bring us back to the root, because many people lost themselves in pursuit of their goals and dreams. They subconsciously or unintentionally become someone else in the long run. People evaluate their businesses, careers, relationships, different procedures, and processes involved in the pursuit of their dreams, but they fail to evaluate themselves. They fail to evaluate their inner-selves. There are habits that when you develop them and make them part of your daily life; it naturally and automatically makes you powerful. It gives you constant inner peace. The idea in this book is to really get people to think deep not just about what they are doing but how they are doing it. The greatest creation of God is mankind. When man can actually figure out or cultivate certain principles of life that will keep them in constant right position with God that will make a huge difference in the universe.

These garbage thoughts; anger, un-forgiveness, pride, selfishness, jealousy, and so on has really damaged the souls of many. Although many might think they are successful in life, but that is not all that matters. The question is how are you doing it? How did you get there? The greatest virtue in life is LOVE; this might be difficult for many because they have never felt loved in their lives. They might have had a horrible childhood or up-bringing; -- abused, molested, hated, or treated with great malignity. I know that's not fair, but you don't have to remain in that shell. You can change, it is very possible. That is why I called this book *Fundamentals to a Fulfilled Life*. Most times, it is very difficult to go back to the root or foundation, but most times that's where the true healing lies. This book is written in simple terms and words and is very short to help us evaluate our habits and ourselves so we can see what needs to be changed. These habits in here are contagious. When you practice them it automatically influences people around you, and maybe you have practiced all these before and you were hurt badly by people you loved and trusted, they paid you evil for your good and that made you turn. That's not fair either, but let me ask you: since you turned, how has your life been going? How peaceful is your spirit? Just sincerely answer it. When you understand that whatever you do in life is for a higher purpose, greater than you and others. You will genuinely learn how to love and forgive. I want to challenge you to observe and evaluate your inner peace and satisfaction NOW! And then practice sincerely what you learned in this book for just 30 days and then carry out another observation and evaluation. Check what changed, Check what improved; both your innovations and effectiveness. I am convinced you will have a testimony. I love you and care about you so deeply. I don't only want you to have the best life could offer, I want you to enjoy it. I want you to enjoy the best version of yourself and life too. Remember you can have some things and not enjoy them; these are two different things. I don't only want you to have it, I want you to enjoy it. I want you to know we are in this journey together, am not there yet, neither am I perfect. But I will be praying for you, and I trust you will be praying for me too. Thank you so much for reading and God bless you abundantly.

# ACKNOWLEDGEMENT

I want to thank the Almighty God, and the Holy Spirit for the inspiration to write this great book. I want to thank my wife and my son for their love and support.

I want to thank some special people and also my team who contributed one way or another for the success of this great book; NnekaChukwudozie, MarivonSama, KayodeFowora, ImuetinyanOmere (IMT), Dennis Shaba. You are all are appreciated.

www.ingramcontent.com/pod-product-compliance
Lightning Source LLC
Chambersburg PA
CBHW052126110526
44592CB00013B/1775